A Mother's Cherished Memories

Featuring artwork by Hélène Léveillée and stories by Cleo Roberson

Artwork is reproduced under license from ÉDITIONS GALERIE L'IMAGERIE LTD and may not be reproduced without permission. For information on the art prints featured in this book, write to:
ÉDITIONS GALERIE L'IMAGERIE LTD
795 côte d' Abraham
Quebec City, Quebec G1R 1A2 Canada

For licensing information, contact
Evergreen Ideas, Inc.
(615) 826-6775

This book produced by Evergreen Ideas, Inc., in association with Creative Source and ÉDITIONS GALERIE L'IMAGERIE LTD Special thanks to Jan Anderson, Donna Richardson, Guy Laberge, and Marie-Nicole Néron.

This edition published by Honor Books, P.O. Box 55388, Tulsa, Oklahoma 74155

Printed and bound in Indonesia by APP Printing

ISBN 1-56292-985-3

01 02 03 04 05 06 07 08 09 10 /TK/ 10 9 8 7 6 5 4 3 2 1

Contents

A Mother's Cherished Memories

Our Family's Story

Illustrations by Hélène Léveillée

Stories by Cleo Roberson

HONOR BOOKS

A Mother's Cherished Memories

It would be so simple if we could just capture each special moment of our children's lives with a net. Once captured, we could confine the memories in a special closet and bring them out one by one when we have the time to put them in their own special places. The problem is there is no such net, so like other treasured traditions, it falls to mothers to see that the memories of today are somehow captured and secured for their children's tomorrows.

A Mother's Cherished Memories was written to help you capture the precious moments of your family's life. Holidays past, family births, and weddings will come to life as each page is filled with your own special celebrations and life stories.

Those memories give children a glimpse into family, a sense of belonging, and a feeling of continuity. And long after our children have become adults and parents themselves, the recorded memories will become precious, tangible reminders of how much they were loved and cherished.

The

The
Apple
Tree

We have a family tree. All families do, it's just that ours is growing in the backyard. All family trees start out as seedlings. Ours began when Curt, our four-year-old, decided to plant the seeds of "the best apple he had ever tasted." In fact, we planted three of those apple seeds in glass jars. We sat the containers under a desk light on a chest of drawers where Curt and his six-year-old brother, Bry, could safely reach them and take turns watering them. We watched the jars with great anticipation for any signs of life, and were finally rewarded with the appearance of tiny green shoots. We had baby apple trees! We were all amazed.

I mentioned our "orchard" experiment to some friends at work and was very quickly told by an uninvited listener that if the trees should live, they would never bear fruit because the apples were hybrids. I didn't know what that meant, nor did I really care. We had apple trees growing in our sons' bedroom and surely that meant we would have apples. . .eventually.

When the trees were about a foot tall, my parents took one home with them. Being excellent gardeners and caretakers they planted the tree, fertilized it, and placed a piece of drainage tile at its base to funnel water and nutrients to it. The remaining two trees were left in our not so meticulous care to struggle on in their pots.

Three years later my parents presented Curt with a five-foot tall apple tree to plant in the backyard. Our two trees were dwarfed by comparison. The one my parents had cared for was sturdy and straight.

My father gave us detailed instructions on tree care and pruning. We didn't do any of it, but we did water them. We watched the trees grow, year by year. The one my parents had started was always the biggest, but

none of them ever showed any signs of blooming. I talked to a few agronomists over the years and they told me it was possible that the trees would bear fruit, but that it would probably take a very long time. And still we watched. When Bry graduated from high school and left for college, we still had no apples. Two years later, when our youngest son was a senior in high school, I noticed the blooms. There were actually twelve blooms on the biggest apple tree.

It had taken fourteen years for Curt's tree to bloom and bear apples. His child-like faith in the ability to have wonderful apples from the seeds he planted had been rewarded. He was very pleased with himself and his apple tree. Of course, "his" apple tree had belonged to all of us through the years. My father was quick to point out whose tree it was that had the first apples, but it was of no consequence and it was of no question to Curt. It had been his idea, and so it was his tree.

My father died that same year, but he lived long enough to see "his" apple tree bloom, and to argue with his youngest grandson about ownership of the prolific tree.

The trees continued to grow. Year after year we ate fresh apples. Friends took apples for their horses and we gave apples to the neighborhood children. The birds and the squirrels got their share of apples and we still had many to share.

Our grandchildren now eat apples every summer from the tree that started as only a seed of faith. They do not know yet that they are partaking of fruits of faith. But, in time, they will hear the story and they will understand for themselves. From a small boy and a few tiny little seeds came a testament to what real faith is: the substance of things hoped for, the evidence of things not seen (Hebrews 11:1). And that is how our family tree came to be.

Our Family Tree

Mom's Family

_____   _____
Grandmother   Grandmother

_____   _____
Grandfather   Grandfather

_____
Mom

_____
Dad

_____

_____
Sisters

_____

_____
Brothers

Dad's Family

_____
Grandmother

_____
Grandmother

_____
Grandfather

_____
Grandfather

_____
Mom

_____
Dad

_____

_____
Sisters

_____

_____
Brothers

Our Family

Mom

_____

Dad

_____

_____

_____

Sisters

_____

_____

_____

Brothers

Family Records

_____

_____

_____

_____

_____

_____

_____

_____

_____

_____

Hold On Tight

Héline Léveillée

For nine months this baby had been growing under my heart, then came the painful separation as one body became two. I had no idea at the moment of birth that this first separation was just the beginning of learning to let go, learning how to not hold on so tightly.

As mothers we spend our whole lives holding on to our children. Just moments after birth, we hold that precious little one and a tiny hand grasps our finger and holds on. That newly emerged part of us then snuggles up against our heart, searching for that sound which has become synonymous with life and love. This is the first time the new arrival is held tightly, on the outside, and we speak the words which are to be repeated so many times throughout our lives: "Hold on tight, hold on tight to us," we whisper. "Don't ever let go."

We could not bear it if they should ever let go too soon. "Hold on tight," we say, while helping them to take the first of many faltering steps.

"Hold on tight," we whisper
as they wrap those little arms
around our necks and we
carry them off to bed.

"Hold on tight," we whisper, as they wrap those little arms around our necks and we carry them off to bed.

"Hold on tight," we caution, as they ask us to push them higher and higher in the swing, or as they beg to go faster and faster on the merry-go-round.

We continue to hold on tightly to their hands through every major event in their lives. We hold them when they are sick or hurt, and while they get their first shots. We hold them while surviving the loss of dear pets and through the heartbreak of losing their first love. We hold them during scary movies and through all the scary moments that come with being a parent.

As we hold those little hands, we wonder where the future will take them. We hope the world will be kind to them and we pray they will be kept safe from harm. But even as we hold on for as long as we can, we know that there will be a season for letting go.

So as they grow to need us less and less, we must take comfort in the knowledge that we have done our jobs. We must take all of those memories from every single moment and hold on tightly to

A Mother's Prayer

Her bond will last forever
With every child she bears
And that is something special
Only she and I will share.

For every child that's sent to Earth
Will have started out with me
And I must entrust them
To a special entity.

So I will make a mother
Endowed with special prayer
When she needs my help
She can reach me anywhere.

I will give her the touch of angels
And words of wisdom to share
She will only have to ask
And I will be right there.

A mother's prayer will reach me
In heaven up above
I will always hear a mother's prayer
For it is always sent with love.

Hélène Léveillée

them. A mother's cherished memories are stored away in a special place in her heart, and it's there that we know our children will always be with us. And if we are lucky, they will have made a special place in their hearts filled with cherished memories, too.

When We Were Babies

Mom's name _____

Mom's birthday is on the _____ day of _____

When mom was born she weighed _____ and was _____ in length. She had _____ hair and her eyes were _____.

As a baby, mom's favorite toys were: _____

_____

_____

_____

The following were mom's favorite lullabies and bedtime stories:

_____

_____

_____

_____

Dad's name_____

Dad's birthday is on the _____ day of _____

When dad was born he weighed _____ and was _____ in
length. He had _____ hair and his eyes were _____.

As a baby, dad's favorite toys were: _____

_____

_____

_____

The following were dad's favorite lullabies and bedtime stories:

_____

_____

_____

_____

Our family has _____ children.

Child's Name _____

Birthday _____/_____/_____

Weight_____Length_____

Place of birth _____

Color of eyes _____

_____

Color of hair_____

A special ceremony for _____was held at _____

_____.

The ceremony took place on _____/_____/_____

Child's Name _____

Birthday _____/_____/_____

Weight_____Length_____

Place of birth _____

Color of eyes _____

_____

Color of hair_____

A special ceremony for _____was held at _____

_____.

The ceremony took place on _____/_____/_____

When We Were Babies

Child's Name _____

Birthday _____/_____/_____

Weight_____Length_____

Place of birth _____

Color of eyes _____

_____

Color of hair_____

A special ceremony for _____was held at _____

_____.

The ceremony took place on _____/_____/_____

Child's Name _____

Birthday _____/_____/_____

Weight_____Length_____

Place of birth _____

Color of eyes _____

_____

Color of hair_____

A special ceremony for _____was held at _____

_____.

The ceremony took place on _____/_____/_____

Sometimes the only way we would go to sleep was if someone sang us a lullaby. As babies these were our favorite lullabies: _____

_____

_____

_____

_____

_____

_____

Mealtime could be a messy occasion for us. The following were our favorite foods: _____

_____

_____

_____

_____

_____

_____

_____

We loved having stories read to us. These were our favorite story books:

_____
_____
_____
_____
_____
_____
_____

We loved to play games. Our favorite playtime activities included:

_____
_____
_____
_____
_____
_____
_____
_____
_____
_____

Humble Beginnings

"Move over!"

"Stop pushing me!"

"That's my food!"

"You're crowding me!"

"You're a pig!"

"Momma, she's pecking me again!"

I was watching a nest of baby birds from an upstairs window as they screeched for food and jockeyed for position every time the parents would land on the nest with a nice juicy bug or worm. I could imagine the entire conversation. The three baby birds had grown so large there was more bird than nest to be seen. The nest was a humble structure of sticks, strings, mud, and paper that had been durable enough to see the little family through high winds and rains during the spring.

Now, any movement or change in position by the nearly grown birds infringed on someone else's territory, and resulted in thrashing, squawking, and more pushing. They had reached critical mass.

Watching this family cope with their simple, but adequate, nest reminded me of the very humble home where we had raised our family. I thought about what a real estate salesperson had said to me when we told her we had decided to add on a family room instead of buying a new house.

"You'll never get your money back out of this house if you do that," she informed us. "This is a cute little starter house, but you need something bigger as your family grows."

But we had decided our money would be better spent adding a room as opposed to financing a new home just when our children would need college funds. So we added the family room. It gave us room to stretch our legs and allowed our children to spread their wings a little more easily.

So our children went from sharing one room to having their own separate bedrooms. They loved having more space, but the arguments didn't stop.

"I didn't say you could wear my blouse! Put it back in my closet where you got it!" one would demand.

"Well then don't borrow my tennis racket anymore!" the insulted one would counter.

And so it went from day to day. We could have lived in the Taj Mahal and it still would not have been large enough to stop all of the arguing. Even the larger family room brought its share of boundary disputes. There were still arguments over which television programs to watch or what music to play. Learning to live together is never easy. We are all individuals with

needs unique to our own personalities. Adjusting to others' needs takes work, and the constant maneuvering for space and position comes to an end only as fledglings leave the nest.

I watched the largest fledgling stand on the side of the nest for three days furiously beating her wings.

"She's getting ready for a trial run," I pointed out to my husband, who was also watching the activity.

"No, she can't be ready. She's too small," my husband worried.

"Well, watch," I repeated. The words had barely escaped my lips when the little wing-beater leaped from the nest and floated to the ground like a weightless leaf.

We watched the little bird hop and glide from place to place for the next week. One by one the others took their leap from the nest, as well. Where once there had been chirping, complaining, squawking and shoving, now sat an empty and lonely nest. But the little nest of twigs, mud, and string had been an adequate starter home for the family who had shared their lives there.

Our children, like the baby birds, had lived in our little "starter house" from the time they were two and three until they left for college, eventually returning with their own families. All our family's needs had been met there. The cycle of childhood to adulthood had occurred there. In that little backyard apple trees, planted by our children's tiny hands, had bore fruit. Grapevines, started from twigs, still hung heavy with fruit waiting to be made into Granny's grape juice. Our little "starter house" had become a home.

It was the home where our children stood on the edge of life and beat their wings until they were ready to fly. It was the home to which they could return for a feeling of comfort. And it was the place they could still be children long after they had become parents.

Last fall we moved from the home where we had lived for thirty years to a house that had belonged to our children's grandparents. As part of the move we included mint sprigs, apple tree seedlings, and grapevine cuttings all from our starter home's backyard. So now we have another "starter house," where we have begun blending memories from the past with the present.

Our Community

We lived in _____

Our family lived here for _____ years.

Our home address was _____

One of the favorite memories from that house was: _____

_____

_____

_____

_____

_____

_____

_____

_____

_____

_____

Community

We also lived in _____

Our family lived here for _____ years.

Our home address was _____

One of the favorite memories from that house was: _____

_____

_____

_____

_____

_____

_____

_____

_____

_____

_____

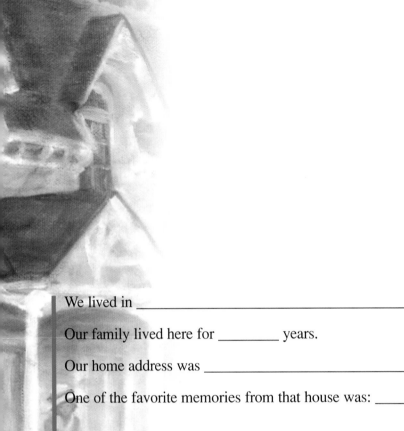

We lived in _____

Our family lived here for _____ years.

Our home address was _____

One of the favorite memories from that house was: _____

_____

_____

_____

_____

_____

_____

_____

_____

_____

Community

We also lived in _____

Our family lived here for _____ years.

Our home address was _____

One of the favorite memories from that house was: _____

_____

_____

_____

_____

_____

_____

_____

_____

_____

We attended _____ church.

Here are a few of our favorite hymns: _____

_____

_____

_____

_____

_____

_____

Prayers were an important part of our family life. This is one of the prayers

we said: _____

_____

_____

_____

_____

_____

Community

These are some of the things we prayed for: _____

_____

_____

_____

_____

_____

_____

_____

Here are some of the special church services we were a part of:

_____

_____

_____

_____

_____

The Security Blanket

It had been a perfect day for a cookout. My entire family of thirteen had managed to rearrange schedules to be together on this beautiful October weekend. Food and fun are always the featured items on the menu at any family gathering, but to a mother it is the memories these events make that are more important. Memories are the essence of any family event and they last a lifetime. And now, with everyone gone, it was the memories past that whispered to me as I cleaned up the all too quiet house.

As I worked upstairs, I picked up two limp teddy bears from the floor. I patted them and put them back into place on the bed. Both bears were devoid of fur in random patterns over their bodies, caused from years of being held tightly by sleepy children. I thought to myself that's just how any good teddy bear should look. One bear was mine and the other one was my husband's. I smiled as I touched the red button nose of my bear. When I was five, my puppy had chewed off his original little black nose. My creative mother had stitched the red button on in its place. I could not remember him looking any other way. I have often looked at the two bears

sitting side by side on the pillow and thought how they represented my husband and me. They are both a little ragged and worn. Their joints bend at odd angles and they have creases where once they were smooth and firm, but they are still recognizable and they still get their job done. A teddy bear's job is to be there whenever we need them and to provide us with the comfort and security we all need. Much like parents, these two teddy bears had remained steadfast. They had stayed behind, patiently waiting until they were needed again.

The next item requiring attention was our oldest son's security blanket. I stretched it out on the bed to look at it for a moment. Our youngest son had a pacifier that gave him the comfort he sought in the night. But, for our oldest, it was the tangible, ever-present blanket that got him through.

The once bright, baby-blue thermal weave was now a pale, almost white soft tangle of string and thread. It was more hole than blanket. It had been patched and re-patched. It was the only blanket that gave our oldest child comfort. Of all the blankets and all the textures that were within our baby's reach, this one had won his heart and trust.

When he was taking his bottle and being rocked, his tiny fingers sought the satin smoothness of a particular soft spot on the trim. With the spot safely positioned between his finger and thumb, he would sigh and start the round and round rubbing motion on the soft surface of the border until his bottle was empty and he fell asleep.

Waking in the night, he would feel for the blanket and turn it around and around until he felt that one special place on its border. No other blanket would do. On one fateful occasion we visited my parents who lived out of town and we left the blanket

behind. Our son was inconsolable. To him that blanket was priceless. It provided him a secure spot in a strange place. It gave him something familiar to hold on to no matter what. Needless to say we never forgot his blanket again.

When the blanket began to take on a transparent appearance, his granny sewed a piece of soft flannel to one side and quilt stitched it all together so the integrity of the texture and border were maintained. The blanket provided security during the first days of school, hard tests, storms, fights, serious and not so serious illnesses, loss of first loves, loss of pets, and it saw him through many dark nights. But through it all, the blanket remained in his room, on his bed. When he left for college the blanket was left behind. He had done a good job of growing up. He had learned to make himself secure. He hadn't needed the security blanket for many, many years but I was glad to still see it on his bed.

A few years ago, when I had the flu, I went upstairs and retrieved the soft remnant of that old, faded security blanket and held it to my face as I sat in the rocking chair. I started feeling better almost immediately. It was amazing. The security blanket really worked. I knew then why he had chosen this blanket out of all the ones at his disposal. Even in its present state, it still had the power to comfort and soothe. Our son had left it behind for us. But he knows where it is if he ever needs it. And he knows that it is safe with us, lying on the pillow between two old teddy bears, providing comfort, memories, and security whenever it's needed.

For when something is truly loved, no matter how tattered, how worn, how torn or how far away it may be from us in place or time, it is always in our hearts and our memories whenever and wherever it's needed.

Childhood Memories

Feelings of safety can come from many things. In our family here are some

of the items that brought us security: _____

_____

_____

_____

_____

_____

_____

These are some of the songs that were sung to calm fears: _____

_____

_____

_____

_____

_____

_____

As a family we liked to read together. These were our favorite

bedtime stories: _____

_____

_____

_____

_____

_____

_____

Our nightly bedtime ritual consisted of: _____

_____

_____

_____

_____

_____

_____

Sometimes after a bad dream: _____

_____

_____

_____

_____

Stuffed animals, tricycles and other toys cluttered our home. These are toys

that held special memories: _____

_____

_____

_____

_____

_____

_____

_____

Playtime was always an active time. These are some playmates who spent a

lot of time at our home: _____

_____

_____

_____

_____

_____

_____

_____

_____

We spent a lot of time at a playground called _____

_____

Most of the time was spent playing on _____

_____

We loved to watch movies. These were some of our favorites: _____

_____

_____

_____

Our favorite television shows were: _____

_____

_____

_____

Here are some of the favorite games that we played: _____

_____

_____

_____

_____

_____

When we ate out we often went to: _____

_____

_____

_____

Our favorite meals were: _____

_____

_____

Our favorite colors were: _____

_____

These are some special treats which we all loved: _____

_____

_____

_____

First Grade

There she stood all smiles and happiness. Who would've guessed just six hours and twenty minutes ago this little bouncing bubble of happiness and contentment had been a sobbing mass clinging to me?

I breathed a sigh of relief as I walked toward my bouncing daughter, who was excitedly waving a handful of papers in the air.

" I had fun! I really did! I have a lot of new friends!" she exclaimed all in one breath.

"And look! I did really well on all my papers!" she announced as she waved them in the air.

I left the school that morning crying softly with my daughter's pleas for help ringing in my ears. This was one of the hardest things I ever had to do, leaving my child behind, all alone on the first day of first grade.

First Grade

I smiled at the wrinkled papers and all the jubilant announcements of new friends and accomplishments. But what I needed most was a hug from my daughter, just a simple gesture of reassurance. Although the first day of school had turned out fine for my daughter, it had been a traumatic one for me.

My daughter, who had so anticipated going to school, had changed her mind once through the school doors. She no longer wanted to be one of the big kids. She just wanted everything back the way it used to be. She wanted to go home, and I had wanted to take her there.

But I followed the teacher's advice to "go quickly" as she pulled the pitiful child from the death grip around my legs. I left the school that morning crying softly with my daughter's pleas for help ringing in my ears. This was one of the hardest things I ever had to do, leaving my child behind, all alone on the first day of first grade. It went against every maternal instinct within me to ignore her fearful cries. This wasn't just a half-day of playtime at day care. This was the real thing; we were to be apart for the entire day. The ties seemed to be breaking and so was my heart. But this time my mind had to overrule my heart.

I looked at my watch a thousand times that day, wondering if time were standing still or moving backwards. It had to be the longest day in history.

But now it was over. We had successfully survived the first day of first grade. It would be good practice for other firsts that were sure to follow. I knew there would be first sleepovers, first camps, first best friends, first boy friends, first cars, and first broken hearts. I knew, also, that my daughter would soon discover that mom and dad couldn't fix everything. But, for now, we just hugged each other and laughed at our triumph. We went home and waited for daddy so the official first grader could share all the excitement with him, too. Soon that first day of first grade was just one memory of the many "firsts" we would share together.

School Bells

_____ began kindergarten
(child's name)

on _____/_____/_____ at _____.

Your teacher was: _____

Your playmates were: _____

_____

_____

You began first grade on _____/_____/_____ at _____

_____.

Your first grade teacher was: _____

Your playmates were: _____

_____

_____

You would get to school by: _____

_____

For school lunch you would have: _____

_____

The following children were invited to your first party:

_____

_____

_____

Your favorite subjects in school were: _____

_____

Your favorite school activities included: _____

_____

These were some of the school trips you took: _____

_____

_____

Favorite school memories include: _____

_____

_____

_____ began kindergarten
(child's name)

on _____/_____/_____ at _____.

Your teacher was: _____

Your playmates were: _____

_____

_____

You began first grade on _____/_____/_____ at _____

_____.

Your first grade teacher was: _____

Your playmates were: _____

_____

_____

You would get to school by: _____

_____

For school lunch you would have: _____

_____

The following children were invited to your first party:

_____

_____

_____

Your favorite subjects in school were: _____

_____

Your favorite school activities included: _____

_____

These were some of the school trips you took: _____

_____

_____

Favorite school memories include: _____

_____

_____

_____ began kindergarten

(child's name)

on _____/_____/_____ at _____.

Your teacher was: _____

Your playmates were: _____

_____

_____

You began first grade on _____/_____/_____ at _____

_____.

Your first grade teacher was: _____

Your playmates were: _____

_____

_____

You would get to school by: _____

_____

For school lunch you would have: _____
_____

The following children were invited to your first party:
_____
_____
_____

Your favorite subjects in school were: _____
_____

Your favorite school activities included: _____
_____

These were some of the school trips you took: _____
_____
_____

Favorite school memories include: _____
_____
_____

Chaos & Clutter

After numerous calls to come to breakfast went unanswered, I decided I would have to go "up there." I took a deep breath and headed upstairs into "no man's land."

As I reached the top of the stairs and scanned the area, I could see no sign of a thirteen-year old, no carpet and only a segment of a bed. My son's entire room was buried under clothes, magazines, shoes, golf balls, baseballs, and various arrangements of blankets and pillows. Tennis rackets and baseball bats lay like crossed swords atop the various piles, holding them in ordered layers, I supposed. Dirty dishes camouflaged his desk, drawing board and bookcase. An attempt to pick up just one plate left me holding a plate . . . stuck to a saucer, stuck to a bowl, stuck to a glass. It was as though they had been fused with some type of greenish-purple, anti-gravity, cosmic super glue. I never knew peanut butter and jelly had that kind of holding power. Chemically-altered gnats erratically bobbed above brown liquid ooze in milk glasses long forgotten. Remnants on other dishes would require identification by a forensic pathologist.

I closed my eyes for a second and a wonderful memory of my son holding our dog, as a puppy, came to mind. It was a refreshing break,

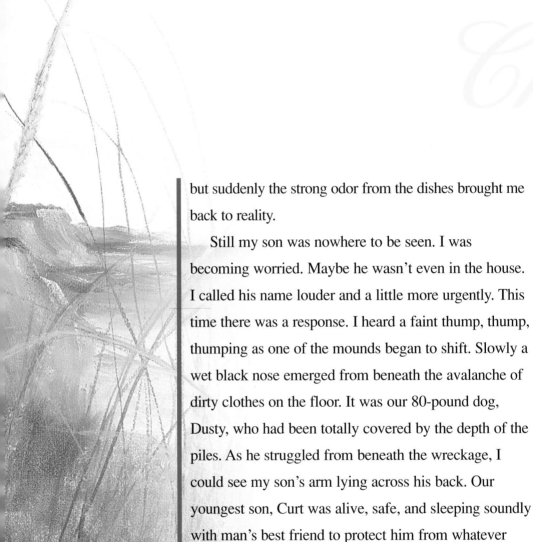

but suddenly the strong odor from the dishes brought me back to reality.

Still my son was nowhere to be seen. I was becoming worried. Maybe he wasn't even in the house. I called his name louder and a little more urgently. This time there was a response. I heard a faint thump, thump, thumping as one of the mounds began to shift. Slowly a wet black nose emerged from beneath the avalanche of dirty clothes on the floor. It was our 80-pound dog, Dusty, who had been totally covered by the depth of the piles. As he struggled from beneath the wreckage, I could see my son's arm lying across his back. Our youngest son, Curt was alive, safe, and sleeping soundly with man's best friend to protect him from whatever might lie buried in those dangerous mounds.

I breathed a sigh of relief and retreated back down the stairs. Curt was a gifted artist and athlete. He was also a handsome, decent, funny, generous, and enjoyable human being. And like many creative people, he was creative with his living arrangements and fashion statements. So after years of arguing about the condition of his room, he and I had established a truce, of sorts. We had agreed that unless I ran out of dishes, I was not to ransack his room. We had also agreed that I was not to disturb his clothes piles looking for clothes to wash. He insisted there was order in his chaos and my shuffling through it destroyed his workable system. In return, he would bring down the dishes at least once a week and he would wash his own clothes or, at least, wear the cleanest of his dirty garments. We further agreed he would actually clean his room under three conditions: 1) If he had company over, 2) If odors

began to bother other family members, 3) If buzzards began to circle the house.

Some people could not have lived with that agreement. But I had put a lot of thought into it, and had come to the conclusion that his room was to remain out of sight. I didn't have to look at it, he did. It was his room and the beginning of personal responsibilities for him. Life was too short and time too precious to waste arguing about something that would change in time anyway. It was more important to me that our communications not always involve a list of things he should do to his room.

And, on occasion, when those terrible mental images of his room would flash before me, I would quickly replace them with the image of his smiling face. I would picture his shy grin anytime someone gave him a compliment on his artwork or some sports achievement. I would remember his gentleness and patience with children. He was respectful to his elders and he loved animals and nature. Yes, there was a lot more positive than negative about our youngest son. And if he could not be house-trained just yet, maybe some understanding wife could do it years down the road. I would tell her that I tried. But I would have to admit to her that I had failed and now it would be up to her to tame his artistic soul. But that would come in time. I had the here and now to learn from and to enjoy. I just wouldn't worry about his room at all, unless. . .those buzzards began to circle.

The Wonder Years

_____ wanted to be a _____
        (child's name)

_____ when _____ grew up.

You graduated from _____ Middle School on ____/____/____.

The family members who were in attendance were: _____
_____
_____

Your favorite classes were: _____
_____

Your favorite teachers were: _____
_____

You attended _____ High School and graduated on ____/____/____.

The family members who were in attendance were: _____
_____
_____

These were your friends in high school: _____
_____
_____

Your best friend was: _____
_____

As a teenager you liked to listen to: _____

_____

You played the following sports: _____

_____

You played these instruments: _____

_____

These are the clubs you joined: _____

_____

You competed in: _____

_____

And won these awards: _____

_____

These were some of the school trips you liked most: _____

_____

Your first date was with: _____

You went to: _____

The first school dance you went to was: _____

You went with: _____

_____ wanted to be a _____

_____ when _____ grew up.

You graduated from _____ Middle School on _____/_____/_____.

The family members who were in attendance were: _____
_____
_____

Your favorite classes were: _____
_____

Your favorite teachers were: _____
_____

You attended _____ High School and graduated on _____/_____/_____.

The family members who were in attendance were: _____
_____
_____

These were your friends in high school: _____
_____
_____

Your best friend was: _____
_____

As a teenager you liked to listen to: _____

_____

You played the following sports: _____

_____

You played these instruments: _____

_____

These are the clubs you joined: _____

_____

You competed in: _____

_____

And won these awards: _____

_____

These were some of the school trips you liked most: _____

_____

Your first date was with: _____

You went to: _____

The first school dance you went to was: _____

You went with: _____

_____ wanted to be a _____

_____ when _____ grew up.

You graduated from _____ Middle School on _____/_____/_____.

The family members who were in attendance were: _____
_____
_____

Your favorite classes were: _____
_____

Your favorite teachers were: _____
_____

You attended _____ High School and graduated on _____/_____/_____.

The family members who were in attendance were: _____
_____
_____

These were your friends in high school: _____
_____
_____

Your best friend was: _____
_____

As a teenager you liked to listen to: _____

_____

You played the following sports: _____

_____

You played these instruments: _____

_____

These are the clubs you joined: _____

_____

You competed in: _____

_____

And won these awards: _____

_____

These were some of the school trips you liked most: _____

_____

Your first date was with: _____

You went to: _____

The first school dance you went to was: _____

You went with: _____

Fluffy

She was just a small ball of brown fluff when she came to live with us. Fluffy was an Irish Setter with natural parenting skills. She would turn out to be one of the best pets we ever had. Protective and loyal, forgiving and watchful, she was always on guard to protect "her" family.

Wherever the children and their friends would go she would follow. If they all rode bikes, she would follow along pulling at their socks or pant legs in an attempt to make them stop riding. She hated bikes and wanted the children safely on the ground, on two feet. But if they insisted on riding, off she went beside them.

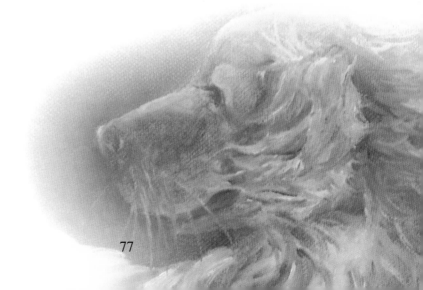

She barked furiously at the mailmen, meter readers, and delivery trucks but never attempted to harm anyone. She was just sounding her alarm of "intruder on the premises." She loved riding in the car with her head stuck out the window and her nose sniffing every new, unfamiliar scent. And she loved children.

One day our youngest son had disobeyed the rules and run into the street after a ball. Even though I was yelling, "No!" and "Stop!" at the top of my lungs, he continued his pursuit. Once he was safely captured, I began to discipline him as a reminder to never run into the street again. At the sound of my child's distress, Fluffy immediately appeared. In an instant she pushed herself between the victim and me. Fixing me with an

intense gaze that left no need for interpretation, she began to
bristle and emit a low, growling sound with her teeth affixed
firmly to my sleeve. I got the message. Fluffy didn't believe in
corporal punishment and I had better see it her way, or else.

When all the children
went to the school
playground, she went too.

Always needing to be
close to 'her' children, she
rode the merry-go-round
with them and walked
cautiously up the steps to go
down the slides beside them.
She was a unique and
special dog.

She raised the children
well. She slept by their beds
at night and watched for
their return every day. Her
tail greeted them with a wag
whether they had been gone
a minute or a week.

They were teenagers when her eyes became dim and arthritis made her movements painful. Yet, still she tugged at their pant legs when they mounted their bikes and still she guarded the premises from intruders. It had become harder and harder for her to keep up with them now that they were older and could travel further. But, with strong determination and love, she still followed only a little further behind.

What she asked was to be loved and cherished. What she gave was all the love and loyalty she had in her heart. Fluffy was a good dog. She taught me a lot about raising children. She was also a good mother, and she would be very proud of how her "pups" turned out.

Loyal Family Friends

Our loyal friend was a pet named: _____

who joined our family on: _____

We chose the name because: _____

_____

_____

_____

We trained _____ to _____

_____

_____

_____

_____

_____

_____

Favorite food and treats were: _____

_____

_____

Our favorite places to play were: _____

_____

_____

Some of our memorable traveling experiences were: _____

_____

_____

_____

_____

_____

A favorite memory: _____

_____

_____

_____

Funniest family pet story was when: _____

_____

_____

_____

_____

_____

_____

_____

These are some of our other pets: _____

_____

_____

_____

_____

_____

These were some of the neighborhood pets: _____

_____

_____

_____

_____

Make A
Joyful Noise

Some of the children's choir members were lined up across the stage in their choir robes. On this special night there were smiling cherubs disguised as cows, sheep, donkeys, the wise men, the holy family and the heavenly host. With smiles on their faces they mooed, hee-hawed, bleated, and brayed. The joyful noises coming from the little barnyard animals were quite realistic . . . and loud. Little hands escaped from the trappings of animal sleeves to enthusiastically wave to familiar faces in the audience. As the noise and barely containable enthusiasm died down, the lights dimmed and the little ones began the Christmas story in songs long familiar to us.

The donkeys' ears were hanging in their faces, requiring a constant flipping of donkey heads up and down to keep their vision unhindered. The little lambs kept wandering toward parents in the audience and had to keep being brought back into the fold by the wise men. The larger cows were bullying the smaller members of the herd, pushing some of them off balance in the process.

The much more dignified angelic members of the heavenly host rolled their eyes heavenward in disgust at the unruly animals and kept on singing. Mary and Joseph paid no attention to the chaos all around them. They were focused.

The annual children's Christmas pageant was in full swing. Parents, grandparents, and friends

sat in the audience watching. They smiled and laughed in unison as the little ones on stage brought to life that moment when God's promise to man was fulfilled in the form of a newborn babe lying in the manger. During the performance I noticed that many notes were off-key. But what struck me even more was that it still sounded like beautiful music to the proud parents and friends sitting there listening. As I sat watching the audience's reactions, I thought how precious each of those little faces on stage was to someone in attendance.

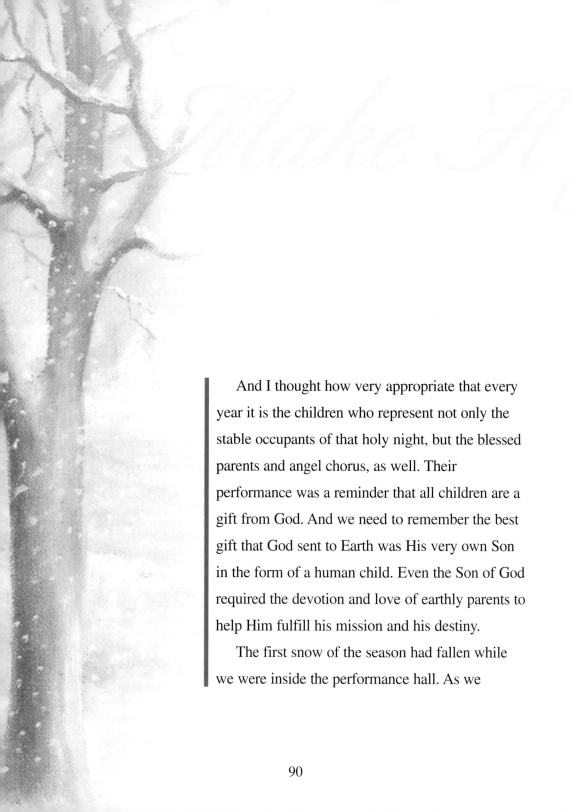

And I thought how very appropriate that every year it is the children who represent not only the stable occupants of that holy night, but the blessed parents and angel chorus, as well. Their performance was a reminder that all children are a gift from God. And we need to remember the best gift that God sent to Earth was His very own Son in the form of a human child. Even the Son of God required the devotion and love of earthly parents to help Him fulfill his mission and his destiny.

The first snow of the season had fallen while we were inside the performance hall. As we

walked to our car I looked toward heaven and gave
heartfelt thanks to God for His child in the manger.
And I also thanked Him for the children he had
given me and the blessings we shared as a family.

Work and Play

As a family we liked to: _____

_____

_____

_____

_____

_____

_____

_____

_____

_____

_____

_____

_____

A special talent for _____ runs in our family.

This is a list of the family members who share the talent: _____

_____

_____

_____

_____

_____

_____

Our favorite hobbies were: _____

_____

_____

_____

_____

_____

To support our family, Mom and Dad worked very hard. They: _____

_____

_____

_____

_____

_____

_____

_____

_____

_____

_____

_____

_____

_____

Mom went to _____ school.

Dad went to _____ school.

Special memories from school include: _____

_____

_____

_____

_____

_____

_____

_____

_____

_____

_____

_____

_____

_____

Our family volunteered at: _____

_____

_____

_____

_____

_____

_____

_____

_____

_____

_____

_____

_____

_____

_____

_____

_____

_____

_____

Our first jobs were:

Mom's _____

Dad's _____

Children _____

_____

_____

_____

_____

_____

Some important lessons learned from earning money were:

_____

_____

_____

_____

_____

Sand Castles

Hélène Léveillée

When our children were young, vacations always seemed to lead us to the sea. There was an instinctive need to find a stretch of beach, sun and palm trees that made us feel like we were transported to a place complete with sailing ships, castles, and pirates. Of course the sailing ships were really small catamarans, the castles were made of sand, and the pirates were just the kids.

On a recent vacation to the beach I watched as little tanned bodies worked feverishly creating masterpieces and collecting treasures of the sea. Buckets, shovels, scoops, pitchers of saltwater, seaweed, sticks, and seashells were strewn about the building site and grabbed, as the master builders needed them to raise and embellish their fortress.

On a palette of sand they work together in harmony. There were turrets to hold stick flags and moats to contain the sea monsters that swam around the castle. The deep windows were carved with plastic spoons to afford the castle dwellers rooms with a view of the ocean. Steep steps curved gracefully around

the outside castle wall leading to the top. It was indeed a wonderful
structure. Seagulls landed close by to admire the finished product
and to check for any unclaimed crackers. Brown pelicans flew
overhead and admired the grand palace.

Long before the children were ready, it was time to stop. They
reluctantly left their handiwork to obey parental whims regarding
the need for lunches and naps. There was one last viewing of the
fortress before abandonment. Their mothers and fathers "oohed"
and "aahed" over the steps leading to the top of the castle even
though they might be a little uneven and crumbling. The moms and

dads complimented the fine turret work even though the turrets all leaned a little to the right and a lot to the left. The appreciative parents admired the moat work even though the barrier wall no longer contained the water that had leaked into the middle of the castle, creating an unintentional indoor swimming pool.

The appreciative parents and critics agreed that the scalloped seashells were an artistic touch atop the castle wall even though, to a trained eye, they may have lacked uniformity in height or size. And the lopsided windows provided just the right amount of illumination inside the castle. Yes, the parents all agreed, it was indeed a wonderful castle to behold. And it was. It was a castle of dreams. The children saw it as they wished it to be. And the parents saw it through their children's eyes.

The parents knew something the children could not yet know, for they were too young. They understand that the lives and dreams of their children will often resemble castles in the sand. Some things will improve with time and practice. Some things will crumble. Some things will take great efforts from friends and family to help put it all into place. Some things will have to be completely rebuilt from scratch.

And through it all, the people who love them will admire their efforts and hard work even when the results are not perfect. The people who love them will tell them when it's time to rest and when it's time to begin anew. And the people who love them will believe in their dreams, too.

Their parents already know all life's plans start with a dream. And they know that in life, much like castles in the sand, the children won't get everything right the first time, or even the second. But parents also know that results improve with time, practice, and hard work. And, more often than not, the dreams of little boys and girls do come true. For you see, they were the children on the beach not so very long ago.

Bon Voyage

Our first family vacation was to: _____

_____

_____

_____

_____

_____

_____

_____

We stayed at: _____

_____

_____

_____

_____

_____

_____

Bon Voyage

These are some of the things we did while we were there: _____

_____

_____

_____

_____

_____

_____

_____

This trip was so much fun because: _____

_____

_____

_____

_____

_____

_____

_____

Another memorable family vacation was: _____

_____

_____

_____

_____

_____

We'll never forget it because: _____

_____

_____

_____

_____

_____

106

Our first trip to the beach: _____

_____

_____

_____

_____

_____

_____

Our first family trip by automobile was: _____

_____

_____

_____

_____

_____

_____

Our first family trip by airplane was: _____

_____

_____

_____

_____

_____

Our last family vacation when the whole family was together:

_____

_____

_____

_____

_____

These were some of the special things we did while on vacation:

_____

_____

_____

_____

_____

_____

This is the place where we would like to spend our dream vacation:

_____

_____

_____

_____

_____

The Christmas Centerpiece

It was Christmas. All the children and grandchildren were on the way to our house, along with all the other family members from out of town. I had been busy cooking and baking for days. The last of the decorations were in place and presents were under the tree. The table was set and I had just sat down to take a deep breath when my husband turned on the Christmas carols. The fireplace was emitting just the right amount of warmth and the atmosphere was enchanting as "Over the River and Through the Woods" began to play. It was picture perfect.

I checked the table over one more time and collected a stray poinsettia leaf that had fallen. The table looked great. It looked warm and inviting, just as it had looked for five generations. That table had been at the center of family gatherings for longer than I had been alive. It was a centerpiece with its own story of how it had come to be part of the family.

This particular centerpiece had cost one calf. My husband's 100-year-old grandmother had traded the calf her father had given her on her wedding day for the solid oak dining table. It had sat in the center of family gatherings ever since. It had been a part of holiday and family gatherings for so long that it would be easy to take it for granted, but no one did.

My seventy-eight year old father-in-law was the first to arrive. As he sat at the table that once belonged to his mother, he rubbed his fingers slowly back and forth across the grain of the smooth wood.

Quietly he said, "I've eaten many a meal off this table."

And indeed he had. I knew it must seem strange to him to be sitting in his son's house eating off the first table he ever remembered.

As he continued to stroke the wood, I could see the wheels turning in his head. He was remembering all of the meals he had enjoyed with his mother and father at that same table. And, in a few hours, he would be sharing another Christmas dinner with his family and he would do what he had done ever since I had known him. He would laugh and smile at the little ones. He would watch as little hands smeared mashed potatoes and turkey from plate to table. He would offer words of encouragement as tiny fingers struggled with the mechanics of forks and spoons that missed little mouths more often than they found them.

He would accidentally drop tasty morsels to the waiting puppy begging beneath the table and then laugh as the little ones followed suit.

He would eat his last piece of buttermilk pie for dessert and have his last half-cup of coffee at the table before heading home.

He would stand and rub his fingers over the table one more time before leaving. With a sack of scraps tucked under his arm for his faithful dog he would head out the door. The table had provided him with memories one more time, offering both a link to his past and a bridge to his future. It had provided memories for three other generations that day, as well.

Mashed potatoes and sticky handprints washed off the table's surface, leaving no clue as to the menu of the day. With a clean tablecloth in place, the centerpiece sat in the middle of the room looking good as new in the soft candlelight. It had served the family well for five generations and if things went well, it could be the centerpiece for five generations to come. With more memories to be added and more stories to be shared around it, that old oak table would just continue to be one of the family, at the center of everything.

Holiday Memories

These are some of our special Christmas memories: _____

_____

_____

_____

_____

_____

_____

_____

This is what we did every Christmas Eve: _____

_____

_____

_____

_____

_____

_____

And on Christmas Day we would: _____

_____

_____

_____

_____

_____

_____

_____

Our favorite holiday songs include: _____

_____

_____

_____

_____

_____

_____

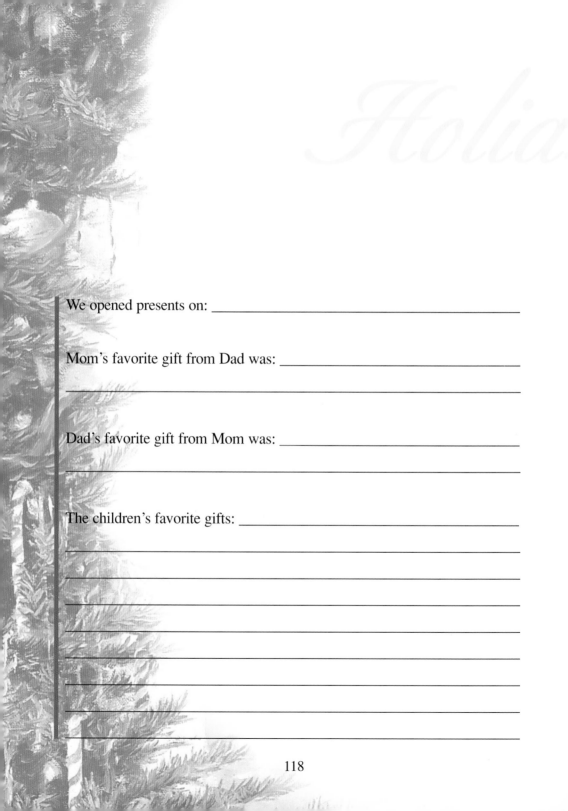

We opened presents on: _____

Mom's favorite gift from Dad was: _____
_____

Dad's favorite gift from Mom was: _____
_____

The children's favorite gifts: _____
_____
_____
_____
_____
_____
_____
_____

We loved to decorate our home for the holidays. Decorating began with:

_____

_____

_____

_____

_____

_____

These are some of the special ornaments and decorations that we used to

decorate our home: _____

_____

_____

_____

_____

_____

_____

_____

We enjoyed having company at Thanksgiving. Here are some
wonderful Thanksgiving memories: _____
_____
_____
_____
_____
_____
_____

We would often gather to celebrate the holiday at: _____
_____
_____
_____
_____
_____
_____

Some of our favorite Thanksgiving dishes were: _____

_____

_____

_____

_____

_____

Other memorable holidays: _____

_____

_____

_____

_____

_____

_____

I Do

I Do

I walked down the aisle on the arm of my
father to the young man waiting at the altar. We
had known each other since we were twelve,
began calling each other when we were fourteen,
and had dated since we were sixteen. Even though
we had dated others in high school and college,
we always came back to each other. And, though
we were opposites in many ways we had a shared
sense of something intangible. It was that
"something" which moved our relationship
beyond simple friendship.

He admired my quick wit, intelligence, and
athletic abilities. I was the only girl he had ever
known that had my own subscription to *Sports*

Love is patient, love is kind. It does not envy, it does not boast, it is not proud. It is not rude, it is not self-seeking, it is not easily angered, and it keeps no record of wrongs. Love does not delight in evil but rejoices with the truth.

1 Corinthians 13: 4-6

Illustrated. I, in turn, admired his intelligence, athletic abilities, and the fact that I could talk with him about anything and everything. We laughed a lot when we were together. And we were on the phone almost constantly when we had to be apart.

During college, I made him cookies and checked on him when he was sick. He walked me to classes and drove me home to see my parents on weekends.

We took care of each other. Through all of the quarrels, accusations, and break-ups there remained that intangible something bringing us back together. We found contentment in each other's presence, and our friendship continued to strengthen.

So, as I walked down the aisle, I walked
toward my very best friend. And, at the altar,
he waited for his best friend. We had found an
identity for that intangible thing. It would
keep us together through our disagreements
and differences, through our pain and our
hurt. Love, though intangible, was what
defined our
relationship. It is
what had always
been there, and,
we knew, what
always would be.

Family Celebrations

Mom and Dad met each other: _____

_____

They got engaged at _____

on _____/_____/_____.

Mom and Dad were married on _____/_____/_____

The ceremony was at: _____

_____

The reception was at: _____

_____

_____

Celebrations

Here are some of the family members who were at the wedding:

_____

_____

_____

_____

_____

_____

A special memory of the day: _____

_____

_____

_____

_____

_____

Our Family Weddings

Bride _____

Groom _____

Wedding Day _____/_____/_____

These family members attended the wedding: _____

_____

_____

_____

_____

_____

_____

_____

Place _____

_____

Bride _____

Groom _____

Wedding Day _____/_____/_____

These family members attended the wedding: _____

_____

_____

_____

_____

_____

_____

_____

Place _____

_____

Bride _____

Groom _____

Wedding Day _____/_____/_____

These family members attended the wedding: _____

_____

_____

_____

_____

_____

_____

_____

Place _____

_____

Celebrations

Our family's birthdays:

_____

_____

_____

_____

_____

_____

_____

_____

_____

_____

_____

_____

_____

_____

_____

_____

_____

_____

A Recipe for Love

The recipe could not have been easier: one box of gingerbread mix, two tablespoons of melted butter, two tablespoons plain flour and one-fourth cup hot water. Stir until thoroughly mixed and roll out onto a floured surface. Cut into desired shapes one-quarter inch thick and bake on an ungreased cookie sheet at 375 degrees for eight minutes. This was not the gingerbread recipe my grandmother had always made for me, but I knew this one would do.

With the five little ones at my house for their pre-Christmas visit I would just use three boxes of mix, triple the additional ingredients, divide the cookie cutters into two separate piles on each end of the table, and let the fun begin.

Like a lot of things in my life, the cookie adventure was much more simple in theory than in principle. After the three batches of dough were mixed and ready for distribution, I placed all the children at strategic positions around the big oak table in the kitchen. The table was over eighty years old and very sturdy. I knew it could handle a few children, some gingerbread dough and cookie cutters.

I made sure there was plenty of elbow room for everyone and that there was nothing sharper than raisins lying loose for additional adornments. Then the fun began. I found out quickly enough that the children didn't need me to roll out the dough for them. They decided that banging on the dough balls with their hands would work just as well. And it did. It also caused a slight problem with the uniformity of the cookies thickness, but I figured that I could just keep removing the "crispy" ones from the baking sheet and putting the others back in the oven until they were done. So the fun continued and the flour flew. The exchange of cookie cutters around the table sounded like jars of bolts and nuts rolling across a floor. The activity was frantic, but productive.

The children had followed my instructions to a "T" about flouring the table surface before patting out any more cookies. However, their zealousness caused some environmental concerns involving the amount of white residue escaping up the chimney of the family room and into the neighborhood. It appeared that the first snowfall had begun a little early that year, inside and out. Three-year-old Jake and four-year-old Katie had really gotten into the swing of dipping the cookie cutters into the loose flour to keep the dough from sticking to the cutters. In fact, they were having so much fun making impressions in the flour piles with their cutters that they stopped cutting cookies and just started making flour designs on the table. Evan, the mature nine-year-old of the group, and Nick, age seven, concentrated on perfection. This was serious

business to them, and they refused help. They assured me they were perfectly capable of doing it themselves. Mollie, Evan's six-year-old sister and an experienced cook with an easy bake oven all her own, informed me that the boys had just dumped "about a pound" of flour on the floor. I didn't know how she could tell. We were standing about ankle deep in flour all around the table. I assured her we could sweep it up just as soon as we finished, or maybe use an industrial strength vacuum.

I took one look at Jake and Katie and burst out laughing. The clouds of flour had finally cleared to reveal their white powdered faces and eyelids, shirts and arms. They looked like giant versions of the cutout snowmen on the cookie sheets.

Mollie was the cleanest, but flour still clung to her cheeks and shirt. She looked like an angelic overseer of the cookie world. Nick and Evan looked as though they had struggled through a blizzard to reach their destination. Only the dog sled was missing.

But there was no fussing or fighting. There was just laughing and sharing and compliments to each other regarding what a good job they had done, and all without any help.

When the last of the dough had been formed into gingerbread creations, I gave them a toothpick so they could make holes in the top of their cookies. They would use this for hanging ribbons in their cookie when the baking was complete.

While the cookies were baking, clean up took place so that the children, table and floor were once again easily recognizable. Jake and Katie slipped red ribbons through the pre-punched holes on the cooled cookies. Mollie, Evan and Nick tied the loops in the strings and then the knots to secure them. They all took turns placing the hooks through the ribbons and hanging their tasty ornaments on the tree.

One lonely branch on the bottom of the tree held ten cookies in a row. That was the row Jake and Katie could reach the easiest.

Mollie, Evan and Nick worked harder at spreading their ornaments around a little more evenly. When they finished, they stood back to admire their handiwork and agreed they had never seen a prettier tree.

It was a sight to behold. Gingerbread men, Christmas trees, snowmen, boys and girls, camels, stockings and stars adorned the tree like understated jewels.

The recipe was a hit. And it could not have been simpler. The ingredients it didn't list however were probably the most important of all: time, a sturdy table, lots of elbowroom, and an abundance of children's laughter and love. These ingredients will always be a part of a favorite family recipe handed down from generation to generation.

Making Memories

Our favorite family recipes: _____

_____

_____

_____

_____

_____

_____

_____

_____

_____

_____

_____

_____

_____

_____

_____

_____

Our favorite family recipes: _____

_____

_____

_____

_____

_____

_____

_____

_____

_____

_____

_____

_____

_____

_____

_____

_____

_____

Our favorite family recipes: _____

_____

_____

_____

_____

_____

_____

_____

_____

_____

_____

_____

_____

_____

_____

_____

_____

_____

_____

Our favorite family recipes: _____

_____

_____

_____

_____

_____

_____

_____

_____

_____

_____

_____

_____

_____

_____

_____

_____

_____

The Snow Angel

Héline Léveillée

It was Katie's first snowfall and she was away from home spending the week with us. We were going to have to do our best to make sure it was a memorable first. Luckily just a few weeks before, her cousin Mollie had provided us with hand-me-down boots and a snowsuit that would just fit Katie. She was excited beyond words. Our little blonde, blue-eyed girl couldn't wait to get "out there" and enjoy the piles of white fluff covering everything.

She stood on the patio, ankle deep in snow, with the snowflakes falling all around her. I demonstrated the art of snowflake catching with the mouth open and head back. She followed suit by tilting her tiny blonde head backwards and opening her mouth heavenward. The snowflakes landed everywhere but in her mouth; they landed on her nose and her cheeks, and they landed on her forehead and her eyelids. Her long eyelashes were covered in no time and her blonde bangs were now frosted white.

"I can't taste them!" she complained.

"Keep trying!" I encouraged.

"What are they s'posed to taste like?" she asked.

That's a good question. Exactly how does one explain what a snow flake tastes like I wondered?

"Well, mostly like a tiny little drop of cold, wet water," I replied.

"You mean like a drop of them 'honey-suck-ems' I tasted last summer?" she asked.

"Exactly," I responded. "Except they won't be sweet, just a little wet." I was remembering how hard we had worked at getting the little drops of honeysuckle sweetness to land on her tongue. She had really enjoyed that tasty treat. The snowflakes finally found their target. She smiled.

"These taste really good," she exclaimed, less than enthusiastically. "But I think I'm already full." Hmmm, I thought. I never knew snowflakes could fill someone up that quickly, but she was little.

"My mouth's gettin' pretty tired," she offered as an explanation.

She had been holding her little head back and her mouth open a long time for a three and a half-year-old.

"Okay, let's not eat too many. We won't have room for supper," I agreed.

"Let's try something different," I suggested. "Let's make snow angels."

Taking her hand we tromped further into the back yard, into a larger clearing away from trees and bushes.

"Watch me," I instructed, as I lay down on my back in the snow and went through the motions of making a snow angel. She was delighted and hopping up and down ready for her turn. Once she was in place, at an arm's distance from my angel, I turned her loose to make her own angel.

She laughed at the motion and the activity. This was much more fun than standing still trying to catch little drops of water on her tongue. When we finished, we stood on top of a picnic table to admire our snow angels from above. There they were, side by side. She was impressed.

"We're big and little angels," she observed, astutely. "And it looks like we're flying."

"You are exactly right," I agreed, enthusiastically. "Do you want to make some more?"

"No, let's do sumpin' else in the snow."

She had found a new medium for play and wanted to be sure she had exhausted every possibility for its use.

147

"Let's walk," she suggested. "Round and round."

So walk we did. Lifting boots heavy with snow we explored a wonderland completely new and foreign to her. Every handful of snow became a ball to be tossed at her granddad. Each tree looked different than it had in the summer, as did each bush. The roofs of houses, birdfeeders, and squirrel boxes were piled high with white frosting. The favorite old tire swing had been transformed into a circle of snow, suspended by an invisible rope. Each footstep left a cratered impression as evidence of the path she had chosen. The rows of tall pine trees in the neighboring yards were now majestic white mountain ranges, reaching from valley to valley beckoning her to come explore.

She was enthralled how the snow had transformed this world into a winter wonderland. I was enthralled with her. I was getting to see snow again for the first time, through her eyes and it was an awesome thing. Everything was new again because of her. The snow had provided me with a temporary wonderland of my very own. This was only one of the many gifts that children give. They make us all young again for a little while. And I had my very own little snow angel to thank for that.

Our Family Stories

There are always family stories that get repeated year after year.

Here are a few of our family stories worth remembering and retelling:

_____

_____

_____

_____

_____

_____

_____

_____

_____

_____

_____

_____

_____

_____

Our family stories: _____

_____

_____

_____

_____

_____

_____

_____

_____

_____

_____

_____

_____

_____

_____

_____

_____

_____

_____

Our family stories: _____

_____

_____

_____

_____

_____

_____

_____

_____

_____

_____

_____

_____

_____

_____

_____

_____

Our family stories: _____

_____

_____

_____

_____

_____

_____

_____

_____

_____

_____

_____

_____

_____

_____

_____

Our family stories: _____

_____

_____

_____

_____

_____

_____

_____

_____

_____

_____

_____

_____

_____

_____

_____

_____

_____

Our family stories: _____

_____

_____

_____

_____

_____

_____

_____

_____

_____

_____

_____

_____

_____

_____

_____

_____

_____

_____

Life's Treasures

Gibberish: My computer screen was filled with unidentified foreign objects, UFOs of the computer world. It was maddening and frustrating! Where there should have been nicely formed letters and symbols there were only boxes, Y's and Z's. That gibberish represented four years of my work copied from floppy disks to my newly formatted computer. I was looking at the screen of Babel.

My very own stories were as foreign to me as hieroglyphics on an Egyptian tomb and about as accessible as a pharaoh's treasure. But these stories were my treasure, put together word by word as thoughts and memories mingled to give form and voice to my family's history.

So now I had to figure a way around the problem. I know that God sends lessons to help us learn and grow. Sometimes they are sent to make us reach out to others. So I did. I called our friend, Danny, who is very accomplished at bailing me out of computer glitches.

He came over and smilingly informed me he could solve the problem in less than a minute. . . and he did. He showed me a few other important procedures then went outside to play with the kids and talk with my husband while I attempted to navigate alone.

Eventually, I got it. The ordeal cost me nothing, but reminded me that we need friends for many different reasons. Sometimes they help us out. Sometimes we help them out and sometimes we all just need to know we are not alone when we have a problem, large or small.

About an hour after he left, I ran into another problem with the screen of Babel in the land of computer hieroglyphics. This time I called my youngest son. The same child who had tried my patience beyond human boundaries as a teenager and young adult, now patiently and calmly talked me through screen after screen and click after click. In less that five minutes he had solved another problem for me. I thanked him profusely for his time and patience with his unskilled mother.

"No problem. Glad to help," he replied.

"How did you get to be so smart?" I teasingly asked at the end of my "lesson."

"Made a lot of mistakes," he answered in his usual common sense brevity.

We both laughed. I thanked him again and we said good-bye.

Later that same day as I sat in the garden reading, my thoughts returned to what Danny and my son had taught me in those brief minutes. If the computer continued to mess up, there were options I could choose to solve the problems. The screen of Babel was just a momentary inconvenience. But even if my friend and my son had not been able to

retrieve my data, I still had the most important things in life. They were my family and my friends. And they were worth more to me than the treasures found in any pharaoh's tomb. It just took a lesson in deciphering foreign symbols to remind me that the real treasures in my life were accessible and obtainable. I just had to take the time to be aware of them.

Words of Wisdom

Our favorite scriptures: _____

_____

_____

_____

_____

_____

_____

_____

_____

_____

_____

_____

_____

_____

_____

of Wisdom

Our favorite scriptures: _____

_____

_____

_____

_____

_____

_____

_____

_____

_____

_____

_____

_____

_____

_____

_____

_____

Famous family quotes: _____

_____

_____

_____

_____

_____

_____

_____

_____

_____

_____

Favorite Family Books: _____

_____

_____

_____

_____

_____

_____

_____

_____

_____

_____

165

Words of wisdom from the family: _____

_____

_____

_____

_____

_____

_____

_____

_____

_____

Words of wisdom from the family: _____

_____

_____

_____

_____

_____

_____

_____

_____

_____

_____

Family Album

Family Album

nily Album

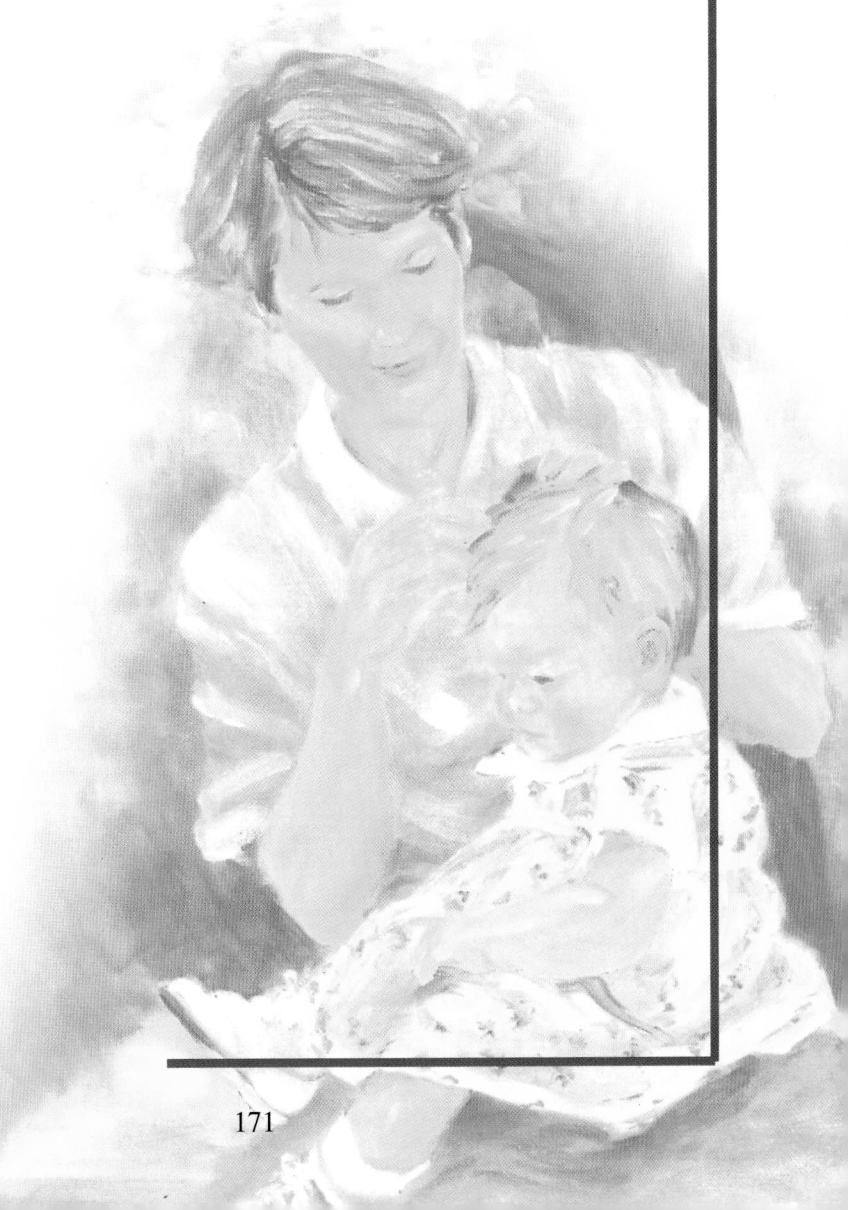

Special Family Memories

Special family memories:

_____

_____

_____

_____

_____

_____

_____

_____

_____

_____

_____

_____

_____

_____

_____

_____

Special family memories:

_____

_____

_____

_____

_____

_____

_____

_____

_____

_____

_____

_____

_____

_____

_____

Special family memories:

_____

_____

_____

_____

_____

_____

_____

_____

_____

_____

_____

_____

_____

_____

_____

_____

Special family memories:

_____

_____

_____

_____

_____

_____

_____

_____

_____

_____

_____

_____

_____

_____

_____

_____

When our life on this earth is over, all we take with us and all we leave behind are memories. How very important precious memories are on all our life's journeys. They give us comfort and sustain us. We are so very blessed to have people we call family and friends to share the journey and to share the memories with us.

Precious Memories